My
FAMILY ESTATE
LEGAL DOCUMENT KIT

LAST WILL AND TESTAMENT,
ADVANCE HEALTH CARE DIRECTIVE,
AND LEGAL POWER OF ATTORNEY

PETER PAUPER PRESS, INC.
WHITE PLAINS, NEW YORK

Our Company

In 1928, at the age of twenty-two, Peter Beilenson began printing books on a small press in the basement of his parents' home in Larchmont, New York. Peter—and later, his wife, Edna—sought to create fine books that sold at "prices even a pauper could afford."

Today, still family owned and operated, Peter Pauper Press continues to honor our founders' legacy—and our customers' expectations—of beauty, quality, and value.

———•———

Thanks to Attorney Susan Colson, of EdwardsColsonLaw, PLLC,

445 Hamilton Ave., Suite 1102, White Plains, New York 10601, for her review of this material.

Designed by Margaret Rubiano

Images used under license from Shutterstock.com

Visit us at www.peterpauper.com

Please note: This product provides basic forms and does not constitute the rendering of legal advice or services. Changes in state law may affect your circumstances. For specific advice geared to your situation and your state's laws, consult an attorney in your state. State law varies and this form was not prepared by a person licensed to practice law in your state.

CONTENTS

INTRODUCTION

This easy-to-use kit is designed to take the mystery out of creating the basic legal documents every family needs. Save time and money on research and legal fees. Understand what it is you're paying an attorney to do for you. Become familiar with what is required in order to make more informed decisions.

Whether you're working with an attorney or doing it on your own, this self-help kit will help you create a **Last Will and Testament**, **Advance Health Care Directive**, and **Legal Power of Attorney**.

Follow the directions and compile the information you need. Fill in each form and take it to an attorney in your state for review, or arrange for witnesses to meet with you to sign, whether in the presence of a Notary Public or not. You must follow the laws of your state. Refer to your state's website or contact your county court clerk's office for specific information.

Please note: This product provides basic forms and does not constitute the rendering of legal advice or services. Changes in state law may affect your circumstances. For specific advice geared to your situation and your state's laws, consult an attorney in your state. State law varies and these forms were not prepared by a person licensed to practice law in your state.

LAST WILL
AND TESTAMENT

LAST WILL AND TESTAMENT FAQs

What is a Will?

Your **Last Will and Testament** is your legal declaration of how you want your property and assets handled after your death. It also states how you want children or pets provided for.

You—the person making a Will—are known as the **Testator**. You have the **testamentary capacity** to communicate your wishes in writing, and to sign your Will before two or more impartial witnesses. The result: your Last Will and Testament, a binding legal document.

Why is a Will called a "Last Will and Testament"?

Many people change or update their Wills as their situations change over the years, with marriage, divorce, children, pets, property, businesses, etc. Each time you revise a Will, you must date it. Therefore, your "Last Will," the most recent one, is the Will that is valid.

How do I make a valid Will?

You can use the worksheet in this section to plan a basic Will; it covers most family situations.

Transfer your worksheet information to the perforated fill-in Will Form included (we provide two copies) to create a simple final Will.

Then you will need at least TWO adult **witnesses** (Note: some states require THREE) who are NOT your beneficiaries and are not interested in your estate. You must state, "This is my Will," SIGN your Will and DATE it in their presence. Note: Your witnesses do not have to read your Will, but they must be adults and capable of signing a legal document.

Does a Will need to be notarized?

No. However, if you and your witnesses can arrange to meet with a **Notary Public** when or after your Will is signed, the Notary can affirm the witnesses' signatures with a separate **Self-Proving Affidavit**. This is an extra step to avoid having your witnesses appear in court after your passing to confirm their signatures and to confirm that your Will is what they witnessed, or to provide written confirmation of same. (It may be hard in the future to locate the witnesses to have them appear in court or provide written proof of your intent.) However, not all states allow this. And a few states allow you to have your Will pre-approved before your passing. Check your state's website or check with your county clerk's office regarding all Will requirements. Should you need a Self-Proving Affidavit, we have provided a sample form you can bring with your witnesses to a Notary for their signatures, and the Notary's official stamp or seal.

Your Will is effective ONLY upon your death.

Your Will must be the ORIGINAL document. Not a copy. Keep it in a safe place. The original Will must be filed to begin the probate process.

- Do not alter it. Do not remove any staples, even when making a copy. In fact, don't make many copies; they may cause confusion if you choose to make a new Will. (If you do make a new Will, destroy the old one.)

- Let your Executor, the person who will carry out the provisions of your Will, know where he or she can find the original. Do not keep it in a safe deposit box.

What if I die without leaving a Will?

You will have died **intestate**, having made no valid Will. You will have no control over how your property is distributed or how children or pets are provided for; everything will be left up to the **intestacy laws** of your state.

What if I want to make changes to my Will?

You may modify a Will at any time.

- If you wish to make a minor change, you may amend it with a document called a **codicil**. This must be signed and witnessed, and kept with the original Will.

- If you wish to make major changes, it is best to make a new Will. DESTROY all copies of pre-existing Wills.

- Review your Will after major life events, such as marriage, the birth of a child, or the purchase of a home.

To make a valid Will:

- There must be **intent**. You intend for this document to be your Will upon your death.

- You **must be of legal age** (usually 18, sometimes 16), and of **legal capacity**, or understanding, to make a Will.

- **No one must influence you or pressure you** to make a Will. Your Will should be free of **fraudulent intent**.

- Your Will must be made **in accordance with state law**. Check your state's website or your county clerk's office for information on making a Will.

IMPORTANT:

- You will need to appoint an **Executor** to carry out the provisions of your Will. Decide on an **Alternate Executor** in case your first choice is unable to serve.

- Decide upon a **Guardian** to care for your minor children in the event that you and/or your spouse can no longer care for them. Decide on an **Alternate Guardian** as well. Meet and discuss this with both persons to be certain each would be willing to take on this obligation.

- If you have pets or livestock, appoint a **Caregiver** and set aside funds for your animals' care.

BEFORE YOU CREATE YOUR LAST WILL AND TESTAMENT

LIST YOUR ASSETS.

Make a list of assets—money or property you wish to leave to family, to other individuals, or to organizations, upon your death. This includes real estate property, bank accounts, insurance policies, investments or retirement accounts, vehicles, collectibles, and personal items such as jewelry and family heirlooms.*

Assets Worksheet

Business _____

_____

Real estate _____

_____

Bank accounts _____

_____

Insurance policies and annuities _____

_____

Investments _____

_____

Retirement accounts _____

_____

Vehicles _____

_____

Collectibles _____

_____

Personal items _____

_____

*You may be interested in Peter Pauper Press's bestselling **Peace of Mind Planner** or **I'm Dead, Now What? Planner**, which will help you gather this vital information in detail in one place. Both planners have the same content; just different cover choices.*

LIST YOUR DEBTS.

These of course include your mortgage, auto or other loans, credit card debt, and so on. Your assets will cover funeral and other death-related expenses. Then your assets will be applied to your debts.

Debt Worksheet

Mortgage ....

....

Vehicle loans ....

....

Personal loans ....

....

Credit card debt ....

....

Other debts ....

....

....

....

....

....

....

CHOOSE BENEFICIARIES.

To whom do you wish to leave assets or specific gifts? Beneficiaries might include family members, good friends, other persons, organizations, charities, and institutions.

Beneficiary Worksheet

Husband/Wife

Children

Siblings

Other family members

Good friends

Organizations

Charities

Institutions

LAST WILL AND TESTAMENT WORKSHEET

This worksheet is for illustration purposes only. Please use the perforated forms that follow for your actual documents.
Follow directions in *blue*. Print or type all information. Do not write in longhand/cursive.

LAST WILL AND TESTAMENT OF ....
Enter your full name.

I, ..., having full testamentary intent, hereby declare
Enter your full name again.

that this is my Last Will and Testament. I hereby revoke all Wills and Codicils that I have previously made.

I declare that I am of legal age, of sound mind, and that this Will expresses my wishes without fraud, influence,

mistake, or duress.

I reside at.., City of ....,

County of ...., State of ....
Enter your full address, city, county, and state.

MARRIAGE AND FAMILY:

I am married to ...., hereinafter referred to as my Spouse.
Enter your spouse's full name.

I have the following Children:

Name: .... Date of Birth: ....

Name: .... Date of Birth: ....

Name: .... Date of Birth: ....

Name: .... Date of Birth: ....
Enter each child's full name and date of birth. List all biological and legally adopted children. Do not list stepchildren,
unless you have adopted them. They can, however, receive Specific Gifts (next page) as Beneficiaries.

If I do not leave property to one or more of the Children identified above, my failure to do so is intentional. *Why this statement? Because if you somehow fail to mention one of your children, they may automatically have claim to part of your estate. If you had a child who has passed away, and that child had children (your grandchildren), list those grandchildren as well, for the same reason. Write (Grandchild) after their name.*

SPECIFIC GIFTS OR BEQUESTS:

If you wish to leave specific items (such as an autograph collection, photography equipment, etc.) to a family member or friend, enter that Beneficiary's name, contact information, relationship to you, and the specific item(s) you wish to leave to them below.

Beneficiary Name: ....

Contact information: ....

....

Relationship to me: ....

Gift: ....

Beneficiary Name: ....

Contact information: ....

....

Relationship to me: ....

Gift: ....

Beneficiary Name: ....

Contact information: ....

....

Relationship to me: ....

Gift: ....

If a named Beneficiary of a Specific Gift predeceases me, the bequest to such person shall lapse, and the property shall pass under the other provisions of this Will. If I do not possess any property listed above on the date of my death, the bequest of that property shall also lapse. *If you do not own that specific item when you die, the bequest WILL lapse and the beneficiary will not receive anything.*

RESIDUARY ESTATE:

I bequeath and leave my Residuary Estate, that is, the remainder of my property of whatever kind and wherever

located, to my Spouse _____, provided my Spouse survives me.
Enter your spouse's full name.

If my Spouse does not survive me, I leave my Residuary Estate to my Children _____

_____.
Enter your children's full names.

If my Children do not survive me, I leave my Residuary Estate to be divided by my state's descent and distribution

rules.

EXECUTOR:

I hereby appoint _____ as Executor of my estate.
Enter the name of the person you've selected to execute your Will.

If this Executor is unable or unwilling to serve, then I appoint _____ as
Enter the name of your Alternate Executor.

Alternate Executor.

I hereby give and grant the Executor all powers and authority as are required or allowed in law, and shall serve

without bond. I direct my Executor will pay my just debts, obligations, and funeral expenses.

GUARDIAN:

If my Spouse does not survive me, and it is necessary to appoint a Guardian for my Minor Children, I appoint

_____ as Guardian.
Enter the name and contact information of the person you've chosen to be Guardian.

If for any reason _____ does not act as Guardian, I appoint

_____ as Alternate Guardian of my Minor Children.
Enter the name and contact information of the person you've chosen to be Alternate Guardian.

Funeral and burial wishes:

_____ I direct that, upon my death, my remains be cremated and all cremation and funeral expenses
Initial if you wish to be cremated.

shall be paid out of my estate.

OR

_____ I direct that, upon my death, my remains be buried at _____
Initial if you are choosing this option.

_____ and all funeral expenses shall be paid out
Enter the name and address of the cemetery.

of my estate.

Signed on this _____ day of _____, 20 _____
Date your Will in the presence of two or more adult Witnesses.

at this location _____ in the presence of the undersigned witnesses.
Enter the location.

SIGNED: _____
Sign your full name.

WITNESSES:

We provide space for three Witnesses, but many states require only two. See page 6 for more information.

As Witnesses, we declare that we are of sound mind and of legal age to witness a Will and that to the best of our

knowledge, _____, the creator of this Will, is of legal age to make a Will,

Enter your full name above.

appears to be of sound mind and signed this Will willingly and free of undue influence or duress.

We declare that he/she signed this Will, consisting of _____ pages, in our presence, as we then signed as

Witnesses in his/her presence and in the presence of each other as Witnesses, all being present at the same time.

Under penalty of perjury, we declare these statements to be true and correct on this _____ day of __

_____, 20 _____, at this location _____.

Enter the number of pages of your Will, and then the day, date, and location of the signing of the Will by your Witnesses.

Have your Witnesses enter their names and addresses and have each sign your Will.

First Witness: _____

Contact Information: _____

Signature: _____

The Witness saw the Testator sign and signed in the Testator's and each other's presence.

Second Witness: _____

Contact Information: _____

Signature: _____

The Witness saw the Testator sign and signed in the Testator's and each other's presence.

Third Witness: _____

Contact Information: _____

Signature: _____

The Witness saw the Testator sign and signed in the Testator's and each other's presence.

NOTES

LAST WILL AND TESTAMENT

LAST WILL AND TESTAMENT OF ....

I, ..., having full testamentary intent, hereby declare that this is my

Last Will and Testament. I hereby revoke all Wills and Codicils that I have previously made.

I declare that I am of legal age, of sound mind, and that this Will expresses my wishes without fraud, influence,

mistake, or duress.

I reside at ...., City of ....,

County of ...., State of ....

MARRIAGE AND FAMILY:

I am married to ...., hereinafter referred to as my Spouse.

I have the following Children:

Name: .... Date of Birth: ....

Name: .... Date of Birth: ....

Name: .... Date of Birth: ....

Name: .... Date of Birth: ....

If I do not leave property to one or more of the Children identified above, my failure to do so is intentional.

SPECIFIC GIFTS OR BEQUESTS:

Beneficiary Name: ....

Contact information: ....

Relationship to me: ....

Gift: ....

Beneficiary Name: ....

Contact information: ....

Relationship to me: ....

Gift: ....

Beneficiary Name: ....

Contact information: ....

Relationship to me: ....

Gift: ....

If a named Beneficiary of a Specific Gift predeceases me, the bequest to such person shall lapse, and the property shall pass under the other provisions of this Will. If I do not possess any property listed above on the date of my death, the bequest of that property shall also lapse.

RESIDUARY ESTATE:

I bequeath and leave my Residuary Estate, that is, the remainder of my property of whatever kind and wherever located, to my Spouse ...., provided my Spouse survives me.

If my Spouse does not survive me, I leave my Residuary Estate to my Children ....
....

If my Children do not survive me, I leave my Residuary Estate to be divided by my state's descent and distribution rules.

EXECUTOR:

I hereby appoint .... as Executor of my estate.

If this Executor is unable or unwilling to serve, then I appoint .... as Alternate Executor.

I hereby give and grant the Executor all powers and authority as are required or allowed in law, and shall serve without bond. I direct my Executor will pay my just debts, obligations, and funeral expenses.

GUARDIAN:

If my Spouse does not survive me, and it is necessary to appoint a Guardian for my Minor Children, I appoint

....

.... as Guardian.

If for any reason .... does not act as Guardian, I appoint

....

.... as Alternate Guardian of my Minor Children.

Funeral and burial wishes:

.... I direct that, upon my death, my remains be cremated and all cremation and funeral expenses

shall be paid out of my estate.

OR

..............................I direct that, upon my death, my remains be buried at ....

.... and all funeral expenses shall be paid out of

my estate.

Signed on this .... day of .... 20 .... at

this location .... in the presence of the undersigned witnesses.

SIGNED: ....

WITNESSES:

As Witnesses, we declare that we are of sound mind and of legal age to witness a Will and that to the best of our

knowledge, ..., the creator of this Will, is of legal age to make a Will,

appears to be of sound mind and signed this Will willingly and free of undue influence or duress.

We declare that he/she signed this Will, consisting of .... pages, in our

presence, as we then signed as Witnesses in his/her prescence and in the presence of each other as Witnesses, all

being present at the same time. Under penalty of perjury, we declare these statements to be true and correct on this

.... day of .... , 20 .... , at this location

....

First Witness: ....

Contact Information: ....

Signature: ....

The Witness saw the Testator sign and signed in the Testator's and each other's presence.

Second Witness: ....

Contact Information: ....

Signature: ....

The Witness saw the Testator sign and signed in the Testator's and each other's presence.

Third Witness: ....

Contact Information: ....

Signature: ....

The Witness saw the Testator sign and signed in the Testator's and each other's presence.

Copyright © 2020 Peter Pauper Press

www.peterpauper.com

Last Will and Testament

LAST WILL AND TESTAMENT

LAST WILL AND TESTAMENT OF ....

I, ..., having full testamentary intent, hereby declare that this is my Last Will and Testament. I hereby revoke all Wills and Codicils that I have previously made.

I declare that I am of legal age, of sound mind, and that this Will expresses my wishes without fraud, influence, mistake, or duress.

I reside at ...., City of ....,
County of ...., State of ....

MARRIAGE AND FAMILY:

I am married to ...., hereinafter referred to as my Spouse.

I have the following Children:

Name: .... Date of Birth: ....

Name: .... Date of Birth: ....

Name: .... Date of Birth: ....

Name: .... Date of Birth: ....

If I do not leave property to one or more of the Children identified above, my failure to do so is intentional.

SPECIFIC GIFTS OR BEQUESTS:

Beneficiary Name: ....

Contact information: ....

Relationship to me: ....

Gift: ....

Beneficiary Name: ....

Contact information: ....

Relationship to me: ....

Gift: ....

Beneficiary Name: ....

Contact information: ....

Relationship to me: ....

Gift: ....

If a named Beneficiary of a Specific Gift predeceases me, the bequest to such person shall lapse, and the property shall pass under the other provisions of this Will. If I do not possess any property listed above on the date of my death, the bequest of that property shall also lapse.

RESIDUARY ESTATE:

I bequeath and leave my Residuary Estate, that is, the remainder of my property of whatever kind and wherever located, to my Spouse ...., provided my Spouse survives me.

If my Spouse does not survive me, I leave my Residuary Estate to my Children ....

....

If my Children do not survive me, I leave my Residuary Estate to be divided by my state's descent and distribution rules.

EXECUTOR:

I hereby appoint .... as Executor of my estate.

If this Executor is unable or unwilling to serve, then I appoint .... as Alternate Executor.

I hereby give and grant the Executor all powers and authority as are required or allowed in law, and shall serve without bond. I direct my Executor will pay my just debts, obligations, and funeral expenses.

Last Will and Testament

GUARDIAN:

If my Spouse does not survive me, and it is necessary to appoint a Guardian for my Minor Children, I appoint

....

.... as Guardian.

If for any reason .... does not act as Guardian, I appoint

....

.... as Alternate Guardian of my Minor Children.

Funeral and burial wishes:

.... I direct that, upon my death, my remains be cremated and all cremation and funeral expenses

shall be paid out of my estate.

OR

..............................I direct that, upon my death, my remains be buried at ....

.... and all funeral expenses shall be paid out of

my estate.

Signed on this .... day of .... 20 .... at

this location .... in the presence of the undersigned witnesses.

SIGNED: ....

WITNESSES:

As Witnesses, we declare that we are of sound mind and of legal age to witness a Will and that to the best of our

knowledge, ..., the creator of this Will, is of legal age to make a Will,

appears to be of sound mind and signed this Will willingly and free of undue influence or duress.

We declare that he/she signed this Will, consisting of .... pages, in our

presence, as we then signed as Witnesses in his/her presence and in the presence of each other as Witnesses, all

being present at the same time. Under penalty of perjury, we declare these statements to be true and correct on this

.... day of ...., 20 ...., at this location

....

Last Will and Testament

First Witness: ....

Contact Information: ....

Signature: ....

The Witness saw the Testator sign and signed in the Testator's and each other's presence.

Second Witness: ....

Contact Information: ....

Signature: ....

The Witness saw the Testator sign and signed in the Testator's and each other's presence.

Third Witness: ....

Contact Information: ....

Signature: ....

The Witness saw the Testator sign and signed in the Testator's and each other's presence.

SELF-PROVING AFFIDAVIT WORKSHEET

This worksheet is for illustration purposes only. Please use the perforated forms that follow for your actual documents.
Follow directions in *blue*. Print or type all information. Do not write in longhand/cursive.

STATE OF ....
Enter your state.

COUNTY OF ....
Enter your county.

The undersigned witnesses, ... ,

.... ,

and .... ,
Enter the names of the two or three witnesses.

being duly sworn, depose and say:

On .... day of .... , 20 .... , in the State of

.... , we witnessed the execution of the Last

Will and Testament of the Testator, ...
Enter the date the Testator's Will was signed, the State in which it was signed, and the Testator's name.

Said Testator subscribed the Last Will and Testament in our presence. We heard said Testator declare the same

to be the Testator's Last Will and Testament.

We thereafter signed our names as Witnesses at the end of such Last Will and Testament, at the request of the

Testator, in the presence of the Testator and in the presence of each other, and saw each other sign such Last Will

and Testament as Witnesses thereto. At the time of the execution of said Last Will and Testament, the Testator

was to the best of our knowledge and belief upwards of eighteen (18) years of age, and in all respects appeared to

us to be of sound and disposing mind, memory and understanding, competent to make a Last Will and Testament,

and not under any restraint. The Testator could read, write and converse in the English language and was suffering from no defect of sight, hearing or speech, or from any other physical or mental impairment which would affect his or her capacity to make a valid Last Will and Testament. Said Last Will and Testament was executed as a single, original instrument and was not executed in counterparts.

We make this affidavit at the request of the Testator, _____ .

The Last Will and Testament was executed by the Testator and each of us, as Witnesses.
Enter the Testator's name.

First Witness's Signature: _____

(Printed Name) _____

Second Witness's Signature: _____

(Printed Name) _____

Third Witness's Signature: _____

(Printed Name) _____

NOTARIZATION

This section is to be completed by the Notary Public.

STATE OF _____ COUNTY OF _____ ,

Subscribed and sworn to before me on _____ day of

_____ , 20_____ .

NOTARY PUBLIC _____

MY COMMISSION EXPIRES _____

SELF-PROVING AFFIDAVIT

STATE OF ....

COUNTY OF ....

The undersigned witnesses, ... ,

.... ,

and .... ,

being duly sworn, depose and say:

On .... day of ...., 20................., in the State of

...., we witnessed the execution of the Last

Will and Testament of the Testator, ...

Said Testator subscribed the Last Will and Testament in our presence. We heard said Testator declare the same

to be the Testator's Last Will and Testament.

We thereafter signed our names as Witnesses at the end of such Last Will and Testament, at the request of the

Testator, in the presence of the Testator and in the presence of each other, and saw each other sign such Last

Will and Testament as Witnesses thereto. At the time of the execution of said Last Will and Testament, the

Testator was to the best of our knowledge and belief upwards of eighteen (18) years of age, and in all respects

appeared to us to be of sound and disposing mind, memory and understanding, competent to make a Last Will

and Testament, and not under any restraint. The Testator could read, write and converse in the English language

and was suffering from no defect of sight, hearing or speech, or from any other physical or mental impairment

which would affect his or her capacity to make a valid Last Will and Testament. Said Last Will and Testament

was executed as a single, original instrument and was not executed in counterparts.

We make this affidavit at the request of the Testator, ...

The Last Will and Testament was executed by the Testator and each of us, as Witnesses.

First Witness's Signature: ....

(Printed Name) ....

Second Witness's Signature: ....

(Printed Name) ....

Third Witness's Signature: ....

(Printed Name) ....

NOTARIZATION

STATE OF .... COUNTY OF

....,

Subscribed and sworn to before me on .... day of

...., 20.............. .

NOTARY PUBLIC ....

MY COMMISSION EXPIRES ....

SELF-PROVING AFFIDAVIT

STATE OF ....

COUNTY OF ....

The undersigned witnesses, ... ,

.... ,

and .... ,

being duly sworn, depose and say:

On .... day of .... , 20.................... , in the State of

.... , we witnessed the execution of the Last

Will and Testament of the Testator, ...

Said Testator subscribed the Last Will and Testament in our presence. We heard said Testator declare the same

to be the Testator's Last Will and Testament.

We thereafter signed our names as Witnesses at the end of such Last Will and Testament, at the request of the

Testator, in the presence of the Testator and in the presence of each other, and saw each other sign such Last

Will and Testament as Witnesses thereto. At the time of the execution of said Last Will and Testament, the

Testator was to the best of our knowledge and belief upwards of eighteen (18) years of age, and in all respects

appeared to us to be of sound and disposing mind, memory and understanding, competent to make a Last Will

and Testament, and not under any restraint. The Testator could read, write and converse in the English language

and was suffering from no defect of sight, hearing or speech, or from any other physical or mental impairment

which would affect his or her capacity to make a valid Last Will and Testament. Said Last Will and Testament

was executed as a single, original instrument and was not executed in counterparts.

We make this affidavit at the request of the Testator, ...

The Last Will and Testament was executed by the Testator and each of us, as Witnesses.

First Witness's Signature: ....

(Printed Name) ....

Second Witness's Signature: ....

(Printed Name) ....

Third Witness's Signature: ....

(Printed Name) ....

NOTARIZATION

STATE OF .... COUNTY OF

....,

Subscribed and sworn to before me on .... day of

...., 20................. .

NOTARY PUBLIC ....

MY COMMISSION EXPIRES ....

ADVANCE
HEALTH CARE
DIRECTIVE

ADVANCE HEALTH CARE DIRECTIVE FAQS

What is an Advance Health Care Directive?

• An **Advance Health Care Directive**, or **Advance Directive**, allows you to express your preferences and have peace of mind regarding health care, in the event that you are incapacitated and unable to speak for yourself.
• It is a legally binding document.

What does an Advance Health Care Directive include?

• An Advance Directive names the person who will make decisions for you if you cannot, your **Health Care Proxy**.
• A Directive also specifies **life-saving treatments** (such as resuscitation or dialysis) that you want—or do not want—should such needs arise.
• Your Directive may also stipulate whether or not you wish to **donate organs** after you die.
• This Directive includes three parts:
  • **Part A. Health Care Proxy;**
  • **Part B. Living Will (Living Trust)** if you wish to have one;
  • **Part C. Execution**.

What is a Health Care Proxy?

A **Health Care Proxy** (also called a **Health Care Power of Attorney**) names someone you trust and are comfortable with to make health decisions on your behalf should you be unable to do so.
• This person may also be called an **Agent**, **Representative**, or **Surrogate**.
• She or he may be an attorney, friend, or family member.
• They should be familiar with your views and wishes related to your health care.
• Having a Health Care Proxy helps you plan for any possible unforeseen circumstances, such as a serious accident.
• You must name an **Alternate Health Care Proxy** in case your first choice is unable to serve.
• Note: **You do not have to name a Health Care Proxy,** if you do not wish one.
• Your Advance Health Care Directive form must be signed by you and your Health Care Proxy in the presence of at least two adult witnesses. Your Health Care Proxy cannot sign as a witness.

How do I create an Advance Health Care Directive?

• **Consider the kinds of treatments you want (or do not want) if you are unable to speak for yourself,** whether through illness or through a medical emergency, such as a serious accident.
• You may wish to **consult your current health care providers** about how your health now might influence your future.
• Consider:
  • **Do you want to live as long as possible?**
  • **Or are you more concerned with quality of life?**
  • An Advance Directive allows you to provide instructions, and then change them as you get older, or if your views change.
  • Questions on the following pages may jump-start your thinking.

Must my Health Care Directive be notarized?

• It depends on your state's laws. You must have at least two witness, or have it Notarized, or both. Check your state's website or check with your county clerk's office.

What should I do after I create my Health Care Directive?

• Give copies of your Advance Directive to your Health Care Proxy and Alternate Proxy.
• Give copies to health care providers to be kept with your medical records.
• Tell family or close friends where copies are kept.
• Note: Keep track of who has copies, in case you revise your Directive in the future.
• Review your Directive and update as needed:
  • If and when your health changes.
  • When new information or treatments affecting your health are available.
  • When you undergo major unforeseen life changes, such as marriage or divorce.
  • If your Proxy or Alternate become unable to serve.
  • Alert your Proxy, Alternate, health care providers, and family as to your revised Directive.

How do I revoke an Advance Health Care Directive?

• You may of course revise your Directive as you get older, if your health changes, and as new information or treatments are available that affect your health.
• Notify health care providers and your Agent and Alternate. Tell them verbally or in writing that you clearly intend to revoke the Directive.
• Destroy all copies of your former Directive.
• Prepare a new Directive and sign and date your Health Care Proxy in front of adult witnesses.

HEALTH CARE DIRECTIVE WALLET CARD

You might want to make a card to carry in your wallet indicating that you have an Advance Directive and where it is kept. American Hospital Association offers a wallet card form online at: https://www.aha.org/system/files/2018-01/piiw-walletcard.pdf. You may wish to print it, fill it out, and carry it with you.

BEFORE YOU CREATE YOUR ADVANCE HEALTH CARE DIRECTIVE

Following are some questions to consider and discuss with family, friends, and health care providers.

Do you wish to appoint a Health Care Proxy to make decisions on your behalf?

❑ Yes

❑ No

• If "Yes," think about who you wish to name as your Health Care Proxy or Agent, and who you wish to name as an Alternate Health Care Proxy.

• Meet with both to discuss whether or not they can serve as your Proxy and to discuss your health care values, views, and wishes.

• Will you give your Health Care Proxy or Alternate complete authority regarding your care? (Keep in mind: If you say "Yes," this would include their consenting to, or refusing, life-sustaining care for you.)

Write down their names and contact information here.

Health Care Proxy: ....

Address and Phone Number: ....

....

Health Care Proxy Alternate: ....

Address and Phone Number: ....

....

Think about specific limitations you might give your Health Care Proxy, and discuss these with him or her. (Keep in mind: Some limitations may restrict your Proxy/Agent's power to act in your best interests.)

....

....

Will you limit the health care decisions your Proxy can make?

❑ Yes

❑ No

If "Yes," what specific limitations will you give your Health Care Proxy?

....

....

Following are some conditions and treatments you may wish to discuss with both your health care provider and your Health Care Proxy:

• What if I become terminally ill? ....

• What if I am in a coma? ....

• What if I am determined to have brain damage? ....

• How do I feel about cardiopulmonary resuscitation (CPR)? ....

• What about artificial or mechanical respiration (a ventilator or breathing machine)? ....

• How do I feel about artificial nutrition and hydration (food and water provided by feeding tube or intravenously/

   I.V.)? ....

• How do I feel about antibiotics? ....

• What if I need a surgical procedure? ....

• What if I require an organ transplant? ....

• What if I need dialysis? ....

• What if I need a blood transfusion? ....

To whom will you give copies of your Health Care Directive?

....

....

....

Will you list a date or conditions under which your Proxy can expire, or will it remain in effect indefinitely?

....

....

....

NOTES

ADVANCE HEALTH CARE DIRECTIVE WORKSHEET

This worksheet is for illustration purposes only. Please use the perforated forms that follow for your actual documents.
Follow directions in *blue*. Print or type all information. Do not write in longhand/cursive.

Part A. Health Care Proxy

I, ..., hereby appoint: ....
  Print your full name.

.... as my Health Care Proxy or Agent.
Enter your Health Care Proxy's name, address, and telephone number.

This Proxy shall take effect only when and if I become unable to make my own health care decisions.

In the event that the person I name above is unable to act as my Health Care Proxy, I hereby appoint

.... as my Alternate Health Care Proxy or Agent.
Enter your Alternate Health Care Proxy's name, address, and telephone number.

Unless I revoke it, or state an expiration date or condition under which it will expire, this Proxy shall remain in

effect indefinitely, or until the date or condition identified below.

This Proxy shall expire: ....
                          Enter the date or condition.

My Health Care Proxy has the authority to make any and all health care decisions, according to my wishes and limitations, except to the extent stated below:

....

....

Enter your instructions regarding limitations. You may attach additional pages as necessary.

When making health care decisions for me, my Proxy will consider actions that are in my best interests, actions that are consistent with discussions we have had, my preferences, my religious or other beliefs and values. My Proxy should also consider the following instructions when making health care decisions for me:

_____

_____

Enter further instructions, if any. Attach additional pages as needed.

Part B. Living Will (Living Trust)

This Living Will is intended to guide my Health Care Proxy and to state my wishes regarding the health care decisions I have indicated below.

I, _____, being of sound mind, make this statement as
Print your full name.

my Directive to be followed if I become unable to participate in decisions regarding my health care.

I direct that my family, my doctors, health care providers, and all others, follow these directions. I understand that these directions will only be used if I am not able to speak for myself.

Life-Sustaining Treatment When Terminally Ill or Injured:

Life-sustaining treatment includes drugs, machines, or medical procedures that would keep me alive if my doctor and another doctor decide that I have a condition that cannot be cured and that I will likely die in the near future from this condition.

I know that even if I choose not to have life-sustaining treatment, I will still receive medicines and treatments that ease my pain and keep me comfortable.

I want to have life-sustaining treatment if I am terminally ill or injured.

Yes _____ No _____
Initial your answer.

Life-Sustaining Treatment When Permanently Unconscious:

Life-sustaining treatment includes drugs, machines, or medical procedures that would keep me alive if my doctor and another doctor agree that, within a reasonable degree of medical certainty, I can no longer think, knowingly move, feel, or am aware of being alive. It is believed that this condition will last indefinitely without improvement. My doctors have observed me long enough to make that decision. I understand that at least one of my doctors must be qualified to make this diagnosis.

I know that even if I choose not to have life-sustaining treatment, I will still receive medicines and treatments that ease my pain and keep me comfortable.

I want to have life-sustaining treatment if I am permanently unconsciousness.

Yes .... No ....
Initial your answer.

Artificially Provided Nourishment:

I understand that if I am incapacitated, I may be given food or water through a tube or intravenously (I.V.) to keep me alive if I can no longer chew or swallow on my own or with someone helping me.

I know that even if I choose not to have artificially provided nourishment, I will still receive medicines and treatments that ease my pain and keep me comfortable.

I want to have food and water provided through a tube or I.V. if I am terminally ill or injured.

Yes .... No ....
Initial your answer.

Other Wishes:

In addition to the directions I have listed on this form, I also want the following:

....

....

....

List any directions not already mentioned regarding your health care.

.... I do not have other directions.
Initial only if you do not have any other directions.

I intend that my Directives be carried out unless I have rescinded them with a new Health Care Directive or by otherwise clearly indicating I have changed my mind.

Optional Organ Donation:

Upon my death:

.... I do NOT wish to donate any of my organs, tissues, or parts, and do not want my Health Care Proxy, guardian, or family, to make a donation on my behalf.

.... I DO wish to donate ANY needed organs, tissues, and parts.

_____ I wish ONLY to give the following organs, tissues, and parts:

_____

_____

_____

Initial one answer and fill in any blanks as needed.

Part C. Execution

Signed, witnessed, and dated this _____ day of _____,

20_____, at _____.
Day, month, year, and location where this form is signed.

Principal (You)

Name _____

Signature _____

Address _____

_____

City _____ State _____ Zip _____
Fill in your full name, signature, and complete address.

First Witness

Name _____

Signature _____

Address _____

_____

City _____ State _____ Zip _____
First Witness's full name, signature, and complete address.

Second Witness

Name ....

Signature ....

Address ....

....

City .... State .... Zip ....
Second Witness's full name, signature, and complete address.

Health Care Proxy

I, ..., am willing to serve as Health Care Proxy.

Signature ....

Date ....
Full name and signature of Proxy; date form is signed.

Alternate Health Care Proxy

I, ..., am willing to serve as Health Care Proxy, if the first choice cannot serve.

Signature ....

Date ....
Full name and signature of Alternate Proxy; date form is signed.

Copyright © 2020 Peter Pauper Press
www.peterpauper.com

NOTES

WORKSHEET

ADVANCE HEALTH CARE DIRECTIVE

Part A. Health Care Proxy

I, ...,

hereby appoint: .... as my Health Care Proxy or Agent.

This Proxy shall take effect only when and if I become unable to make my own health care decisions.

In the event that the person I name above is unable to act as my Health Care Proxy, I hereby appoint

.... as my Alternate Health Care Proxy or Agent.

Unless I revoke it, or state an expiration date or condition under which it will expire, this Proxy shall remain in

effect indefinitely, or until the date or condition identified below.

This Proxy shall expire: ....

My Health Care Proxy has the authority to make any and all health care decisions, according to my wishes and

limitations, except to the extent stated below:

....

....

When making health care decisions for me, my Proxy will consider actions that are in my best interests, actions
that are consistent with discussions we have had, my preferences, my religious or other beliefs and values. My
Proxy should also consider the following instructions when making health care decisions for me:

....

....

Part B. Living Will (Living Trust)

This Living Will is intended to guide my Health Care Proxy and to state my wishes regarding the health care

decisions I have indicated below.

I, ..., being of sound mind, make this statement as

my Directive to be followed if I become unable to participate in decisions regarding my health care.

I direct that my family, my doctors, health care providers, and all others, follow these directions. I understand that

these directions will only be used if I am not able to speak for myself.

Life-Sustaining Treatment When Terminally Ill or Injured:

Life-sustaining treatment includes drugs, machines, or medical procedures that would keep me alive if my doctor and another doctor decide that I have a condition that cannot be cured and that I will likely die in the near future from this condition.

I know that even if I choose not to have life-sustaining treatment, I will still receive medicines and treatments that ease my pain and keep me comfortable.

I want to have life-sustaining treatment if I am terminally ill or injured.

Yes _____ No _____

Life-Sustaining Treatment When Permanently Unconscious:

Life-sustaining treatment includes drugs, machines, or medical procedures that would keep me alive if my doctor and another doctor agree that, within a reasonable degree of medical certainty, I can no longer think, knowingly move, feel, or am aware of being alive. It is believed that this condition will last indefinitely without improvement. My doctors have observed me long enough to make that decision. I understand that at least one of my doctors must be qualified to make this diagnosis.

I know that even if I choose not to have life-sustaining treatment, I will still receive medicines and treatments that ease my pain and keep me comfortable.

I want to have life-sustaining treatment if I am permanently unconsciousness.

Yes _____ No _____

Artificially Provided Nourishment:

I understand that if I am incapacitated, I may be given food or water through a tube or intravenously (I.V.) to keep me alive if I can no longer chew or swallow on my own or with someone helping me.

I know that even if I choose not to have artificially provided nourishment, I will still receive medicines and treatments that ease my pain and keep me comfortable.

I want to have food and water provided through a tube or I.V. if I am terminally ill or injured.

Yes _____ No _____

Other Wishes:

In addition to the directions I have listed on this form, I also want the following:

....

....

....

.... I do not have other directions.

I intend that my Directives be carried out unless I have rescinded them with a new Health Care Directive or by otherwise clearly indicating I have changed my mind.

Optional Organ Donation:

Upon my death:

.... I do NOT wish to donate any of my organs, tissues, or parts, and do not want my Health Care Proxy, guardian, or family, to make a donation on my behalf.

.... I DO wish to donate ANY needed organs, tissues, and parts.

.... I wish ONLY to give the following organs, tissues, and parts:

....

....

....

Part C. Execution

Signed, witnessed, and dated this .... day of ....,

20.........................., at ....

Principal

Name ....

Signature ....

Address ....

....

City .... State .... Zip ....

First Witness

Name ....

Signature ....

Address ....

....

City .... State .... Zip ....

Second Witness

Name ....

Signature ....

Address ....

....

City .... State .... Zip ....

Health Care Proxy

I, ..., am willing to serve as Health Care Proxy.

Signature ....

Date ....

Alternate Health Care Proxy

I, ..., am willing to serve as Health Care Proxy, if the

first choice cannot serve.

Signature ....

Date ....

ADVANCE HEALTH CARE DIRECTIVE

Part A. Health Care Proxy

I, ... ,

hereby appoint: .... as my Health Care Proxy or Agent.

This Proxy shall take effect only when and if I become unable to make my own health care decisions.

In the event that the person I name above is unable to act as my Health Care Proxy, I hereby appoint

.... as my Alternate Health Care Proxy or Agent.

Unless I revoke it, or state an expiration date or condition under which it will expire, this Proxy shall remain in

effect indefinitely, or until the date or condition identified below.

This Proxy shall expire: ....

My Health Care Proxy has the authority to make any and all health care decisions, according to my wishes and

limitations, except to the extent stated below:

....

....

When making health care decisions for me, my Proxy will consider actions that are in my best interests, actions
that are consistent with discussions we have had, my preferences, my religious or other beliefs and values. My
Proxy should also consider the following instructions when making health care decisions for me:

....

....

Part B. Living Will (Living Trust)

This Living Will is intended to guide my Health Care Proxy and to state my wishes regarding the health care
decisions I have indicated below.

I, ... , being of sound mind, make this statement as

my Directive to be followed if I become unable to participate in decisions regarding my health care.

I direct that my family, my doctors, health care providers, and all others, follow these directions. I understand that

these directions will only be used if I am not able to speak for myself.

Life-Sustaining Treatment When Terminally Ill or Injured:

Life-sustaining treatment includes drugs, machines, or medical procedures that would keep me alive if my doctor and another doctor decide that I have a condition that cannot be cured and that I will likely die in the near future from this condition.

I know that even if I choose not to have life-sustaining treatment, I will still receive medicines and treatments that ease my pain and keep me comfortable.

I want to have life-sustaining treatment if I am terminally ill or injured.

Yes _____ No _____

Life-Sustaining Treatment When Permanently Unconscious:

Life-sustaining treatment includes drugs, machines, or medical procedures that would keep me alive if my doctor and another doctor agree that, within a reasonable degree of medical certainty, I can no longer think, knowingly move, feel, or am aware of being alive. It is believed that this condition will last indefinitely without improvement. My doctors have observed me long enough to make that decision. I understand that at least one of my doctors must be qualified to make this diagnosis.

I know that even if I choose not to have life-sustaining treatment, I will still receive medicines and treatments that ease my pain and keep me comfortable.

I want to have life-sustaining treatment if I am permanently unconsciousness.

Yes _____ No _____

Artificially Provided Nourishment:

I understand that if I am incapacitated, I may be given food or water through a tube or intravenously (I.V.) to keep me alive if I can no longer chew or swallow on my own or with someone helping me.

I know that even if I choose not to have artificially provided nourishment, I will still receive medicines and treatments that ease my pain and keep me comfortable.

I want to have food and water provided through a tube or I.V. if I am terminally ill or injured.

Yes _____ No _____

Other Wishes:

In addition to the directions I have listed on this form, I also want the following:

....

....

....

.... I do not have other directions.

I intend that my Directives be carried out unless I have rescinded them with a new Health Care Directive or by otherwise clearly indicating I have changed my mind.

Optional Organ Donation:

Upon my death:

.... I do NOT wish to donate any of my organs, tissues, or parts, and do not want my Health Care Proxy,

guardian, or family, to make a donation on my behalf.

.... I DO wish to donate ANY needed organs, tissues, and parts.

.... I wish ONLY to give the following organs, tissues, and parts:

....

....

....

Part C. Execution

Signed, witnessed, and dated this .... day of .... ,

20................................. , at ....

Principal

Name ....

Signature ....

Address ....

....

City .... State .... Zip ....

First Witness

Name ....

Signature ....

Address ....

....

City .... State .... Zip ....

Second Witness

Name ....

Signature ....

Address ....

....

City .... State .... Zip ....

Health Care Proxy

I, ..., am willing to serve as Health Care Proxy.

Signature ....

Date ....

Alternate Health Care Proxy

I, ..., am willing to serve as Health Care Proxy, if the

first choice cannot serve.

Signature ....

Date ....

Copyright © 2020 Peter Pauper Press
www.peterpauper.com

Advance Health Care Directive

LEGAL POWER
OF ATTORNEY

LEGAL POWER OF ATTORNEY FAQS

What is a Power of Attorney?

A Power of Attorney (P.O.A.) allows you to name an **Attorney-in-Fact** or **Agent**, who can act on your behalf if you become incapacitated, are unavailable or physically away (if you must leave the country for a time), or are somehow unable to manage your affairs. You may also name an **Alternate Attorney-in-Fact** in case your first choice cannot serve.

What is a "Durable Power of Attorney"?

"Durable" means that the Power of Attorney *endures*; it survives your disability and continues to be in effect after you become injured or mentally incompetent.

Does my Attorney-in-Fact need to be a lawyer?

No. The person you choose as your Agent does NOT need to be a lawyer. He or she can be an adult child or close friend. It must be someone you trust.

What does a P.O.A. allow my Attorney-in-Fact or Agent to do?

He or she may manage your property, as well as your financial, legal, and retirement matters, and may pay bills or make gifts on your behalf.

Note: Some states allow for a P.O.A. to include health care decisions; some states do not. This Kit, however, includes a Health Care Proxy option in the Advance Health Care Directive section that covers health care decisions.

Must I pay my Attorney-in-Fact?

You may wish to consider payment if your Agent's duties involve a great deal of time or are complex. Your Attorney may also require reimbursement for expenses incurred on your behalf.

Can I change my mind?

Yes, you may revoke a Power of Attorney at any time through a signed **Revocation Notice** delivered to the Attorney-in-Fact and to other parties who may have copies of the original P.O.A.

Can a P.O.A. take the place of a Will?

No. A Will is still required to address the distribution of your assets. While a P.O.A. survives your disability, it terminates at your death.

Does my Power of Attorney need to be witnessed and/or notarized?

It depends on your state's requirements. Some states require two witnesses, some a Notary, some require both. Some states require that a P.O.A. be recorded with your county clerk. Check your state's website or check with your county clerk's office on all requirements. Note: Witnesses should be impartial individuals over the age of 18, not relatives, health care providers, or others interested in your affairs.

BEFORE YOU CREATE YOUR LEGAL POWER OF ATTORNEY

Consider:

• Who will you appoint as your Attorney-in-Fact?
• Who will you appoint as an Alternate Attorney-in-Fact?
• Are they capable of executing the tasks you need done?
• Will they act in your best interests?
• You should meet with each person and discuss the duties you expect them to carry out. Will they accept?

My Attorney-in-Fact

Name: ....

Contact information: ....

Alternate Attorney-in-Fact

Name: ....

Contact information: ....

What are the tasks you need your Attorney to do?

....

....

....

Will you compensate your Attorney-in-Fact?

....

Where will you keep this document and any copies? The original should be kept in a place your Attorney-in-Fact can access.

....

Name and contact information of any lawyer or other persons who helped me create this form:

....

....

LEGAL POWER OF ATTORNEY WORKSHEET

This worksheet is for illustration purposes only. Follow directions in *blue*. Print or type all information. Do not write in longhand/cursive.

I, _____ ,
Enter your first, middle, and last name.

residing at _____ ,
Enter your full address.

hereby appoint and authorize _____ ,
Enter your Attorney-in-Fact's full name.

residing at _____ ,
Enter your Attorney-in-Fact's address.
as my Attorney-in-Fact (Agent).

If my Agent is unable to act on my behalf, I designate

_____ ,
Enter your Alternate Attorney-in-Fact's full name.

residing at _____ ,
Enter your Alternate Attorney-in-Fact's address.

as substitute Agent with the same general Power of Attorney.

I hereby revoke any and all previous Powers of Attorney signed by me.

This Power of Attorney shall become effective on the

_____ day of _____ , 20_____ .
Fill in the day, month, and year.

My Attorney-in-Fact shall have full power and authority to perform all and every act and duty that is reasonably required or necessary to perform the duties and authorities listed below, as if I had done so personally:

_____

_____

_____

Fill in the Attorney's specific powers and responsibilities above. These might include paying your bills, selling your home or auto, and so on.

The authority of my Agent shall include such incidental acts as are reasonable and necessary to carry out and perform the authorities and duties stated herein.

My Attorney accepts this appointment subject to its term and agrees to perform in a capacity consistent with my best interests.

If any part of any provision of this Power of Attorney shall be invalid or unenforceable under applicable law, such part shall be ineffective to the extent of such validity only, without affecting the remaining provisions.

I may at any time revoke this Power of Attorney by completing the Revocation portion of this form (page 58) or by filing an instrument of revocation in the records of the county in which I reside.

This Power of Attorney shall become effective immediately, and shall not be affected by my disability or lack of mental capacity, except as provided by an applicable state statute.

I indemnify and hold harmless my Attorney-in-Fact from any loss that results from an error in judgment that was made in good faith, save for willful misconduct or the failure to act in good faith under the authority of this Power of Attorney.

My Attorney-in-Fact shall provide accurate records of all transactions completed on my behalf and shall provide accounting records within _____ days if I so request or if a request is made by a designated Monitor acting on my behalf.
Fill in the number of days within which you wish to receive accounting details from your Attorney-in-Fact.

My Attorney-in-Fact shall be entitled to reimbursement of all reasonable expenses incurred on my behalf in his/her duties as my Agent, and may be paid $ _____, or a reasonable sum.

Signed, witnessed, and dated this _____ day of _____,

20_____, at _____ .
Day, month, year, and location where this form is signed.

Principal *(You)*

Name ....

Signature ....

Address ....

....

City .... State .... Zip ....
Fill in your full name, signature, and complete address.

First Witness

Name ....

Signature ....

Address ....

....

City .... State .... Zip ....
First Witness's full name, signature, and complete address.

Second Witness

Name ....

Signature ....

Address ....

....

City .... State .... Zip ....
Second Witness's full name, signature, and complete address.

Attorney-in-Fact

I, ..., am willing to serve as Attorney-in-Fact.

Signature ....

Date ....
Full name and signature of Proxy; date form is signed.

Alternate Attorney-in-Fact

I, ..., am willing to serve as Alternate Attorney-in-Fact, if the first choice cannot serve.

Signature ....

Date ....
Full name and signature of Alternate Proxy; date form is signed.

REVOCATION

This Durable Power of Attorney (Limited) is hereby revoked by my signing below.

Dated this .... day of ....,

20..............................
Complete the day, month, and year of revocation.

....

Principal Signature
Your signature

This Revocation is signed, sealed, and delivered in the presence of:

First Witness

Name _____

Signature _____

Address _____

_____

City _____ State _____ Zip _____
First Witness's full name, signature, and complete address.

Second Witness

Name _____

Signature _____

Address _____

_____

City _____ State _____ Zip _____
Second Witness's full name, signature, and complete address.

LEGAL POWER OF ATTORNEY

NOTES

WORKSHEET

LEGAL POWER OF ATTORNEY

I, ...,

residing at ....,

hereby appoint and authorize ....,

residing at ....,

as my Attorney-in-Fact (Agent).

If my Agent is unable to act on my behalf, I designate

....,

residing at ....,

as substitute Agent with the same general Power of Attorney.

I hereby revoke any and all previous Powers of Attorney signed by me.

This Power of Attorney shall become effective on the

.... day of ...., 20................ .

My Attorney-in-Fact shall have full power and authority to perform all and every act and duty that is reasonably required or necessary to perform the duties and authorities listed below, as if I had done so personally:

....

....

....

The authority of my Agent shall include such incidental acts as are reasonable and necessary to carry out and perform the authorities and duties stated herein.

My Attorney accepts this appointment subject to its term and agrees to perform in a capacity consistent with my best interests.

If any part of any provision of this Power of Attorney shall be invalid or unenforceable under applicable law, such part shall be ineffective to the extent of such validity only, without affecting the remaining provisions.

I may at any time revoke this Power of Attorney by completing the Revocation portion at the end of this document or by filing an instrument of revocation in the records of the county in which I reside.

This Power of Attorney shall become effective immediately, and shall not be affected by my disability or lack of mental capacity, except as provided by an applicable state statute.

I indemnify and hold harmless my Attorney-in-Fact from any loss that results from an error in judgment that was made in good faith, save for willful misconduct or the failure to act in good faith under the authority of this Power of Attorney.

I authorize my Attorney-in-Fact to indemnify any third party from any claims which may arise against the third party because of reliance on this Power of Attorney.

My Attorney-in-Fact shall provide accurate records of all transactions completed on my behalf and shall provide accounting records within .... days if I so request or if a request is made by a designated Monitor acting on my behalf.

My Attorney-in-Fact shall be entitled to reimbursement of all reasonable expenses incurred on my behalf in his/her duties as my Agent, and may be paid $ ...., or a reasonable sum.

Signed, witnessed, and dated this .... day of ....,

20............................, at ....

Principal

Name ....

Signature ....

Address ....

....

City .... State .... Zip ....

First Witness

Name ....

Signature ....

Address ....

....

City .... State .... Zip ....

Second Witness

Name ....

Signature ....

Address ....

....

City .... State .... Zip ....

Attorney-in-Fact

I, ..., am willing to serve as Attorney-in-Fact.

Signature ....

Date ....

Alternate Attorney-in-Fact

I, ..., am willing to serve as Alternate Attorney-in-Fact, if the first choice cannot serve.

Signature ....

Date ....

REVOCATION

This Durable Power of Attorney (Limited) is hereby revoked by my signing below.

Dated this .... day of .... ,

20.............................. .

....

Principal Signature

This Revocation is signed, sealed, and delivered in the presence of:

First Witness

Name ....

Signature ....

Address ....

....

City .... State .... Zip ....

Second Witness

Name ....

Signature ....

Address ....

....

City .... State .... Zip ....

Legal Power of Attorney

LEGAL POWER OF ATTORNEY

I, ... ,

residing at .... ,

hereby appoint and authorize .... ,

residing at .... ,

as my Attorney-in-Fact (Agent).

If my Agent is unable to act on my behalf, I designate

.... ,

residing at .... ,

as substitute Agent with the same general Power of Attorney.

I hereby revoke any and all previous Powers of Attorney signed by me.

This Power of Attorney shall become effective on the

.... day of ...., 20 ....

My Attorney-in-Fact shall have full power and authority to perform all and every act and duty that is reasonably required or necessary to perform the duties and authorities listed below, as if I had done so personally:

....

....

....

The authority of my Agent shall include such incidental acts as are reasonable and necessary to carry out and perform the authorities and duties stated herein.

My Attorney accepts this appointment subject to its term and agrees to perform in a capacity consistent with my best interests.

If any part of any provision of this Power of Attorney shall be invalid or unenforceable under applicable law, such part shall be ineffective to the extent of such validity only, without affecting the remaining provisions.

I may at any time revoke this Power of Attorney by completing the Revocation portion at the end of this document or by filing an instrument of revocation in the records of the county in which I reside.

This Power of Attorney shall become effective immediately, and shall not be affected by my disability or lack of mental capacity, except as provided by an applicable state statute.

Legal Power of Attorney

I indemnify and hold harmless my Attorney-in-Fact from any loss that results from an error in judgment that was made in good faith, save for willful misconduct or the failure to act in good faith under the authority of this Power of Attorney.

I authorize my Attorney-in-Fact to indemnify any third party from any claims which may arise against the third party because of reliance on this Power of Attorney.

My Attorney-in-Fact shall provide accurate records of all transactions completed on my behalf and shall provide accounting records within .... days if I so request or if a request is made by a designated Monitor acting on my behalf.

My Attorney-in-Fact shall be entitled to reimbursement of all reasonable expenses incurred on my behalf in his/her duties as my Agent, and may be paid $ ...., or a reasonable sum.

Signed, witnessed, and dated this .... day of ....,

20.................., at ....

Principal

Name ....

Signature ....

Address ....

....

City .... State .... Zip ....

First Witness

Name ....

Signature ....

Address ....

....

City .... State .... Zip ....

Second Witness

Name ....

Signature ....

Address ....

....

City .... State .... Zip ....

Attorney-in-Fact

I, ..., am willing to serve as Attorney-in-Fact.

Signature ....

Date ....

Alternate Attorney-in-Fact

I, ..., am willing to serve as Alternate Attorney-in-

Fact, if the first choice cannot serve.

Signature ....

Date ....

REVOCATION

This Durable Power of Attorney (Limited) is hereby revoked by my signing below.

Dated this .... day of .... ,

20............................... .

....

Principal Signature

This Revocation is signed, sealed, and delivered in the presence of:

First Witness

Name ....

Signature ....

Address ....

....

City .... State .... Zip ....

Second Witness

Name ....

Signature ....

Address ....

....

City .... State .... Zip ....

Copyright © 2020 Peter Pauper Press

www.peterpauper.com

GLOSSARY
OF TERMS

GLOSSARY OF TERMS

Advance Directive. A legally recognized written document in which a person gives instructions concerning their health care.

Agent. The person you appoint to act in your place, designates a healthcare agent and in a P.O.A. is called Attorney-in-Fact.

Assets. All the types of property that you may own, including real estate and personal property.

Attorney-in-Fact. Your agent, the person whom you authorize to perform business-related or other transactions on your behalf, by signing a Power of Attorney.

Beneficiary. A person named to receive something from a Will or Trust.

Bequeath. An act of giving an asset by Will.

Devise. A disposition of real property by Will.

Durable Power of Attorney. A Power of Attorney that continues in effect after a Principal is incapacitated.

Estate. The assets *owned* and debts *owed* by a person at time of death.

Execute. To formally sign an agreement or other document in compliance with legal formalities.

Executor. The person appointed by Will (if there is no Will, this is called an Administrator) to administer the estate of the person who has died.

Fiduciary. A person having a high standard of care and duty, to act primarily for the benefit of another.

Guardian. A person who is appointed by a court, pursuant to a guardianship proceeding, to make decisions regarding the care of another person. Also referred to as a Conservator in some states.

Health Care Proxy. A legal document that appoints another person as your Agent ("Proxy") to make health care decisions for you.

Heir. A person legally entitled to the property of another upon the other's death.

Incapacitated. To be mentally unable to make intelligent, informed decisions.

Incompetent. A person who is not able to manage his/her affairs, due to mental deficiency (lack of I.Q., deterioration, illness, or psychosis) or physical disability.

Intestate. A person who has died without a Will.

Limited Power of Attorney. A Power of Attorney that limits an Agent's authority to only specific areas or actions.

Living Trust. A Trust that is effective during the lifetime of the creator of the Trust.

Notary Public. A person who is legally empowered to attest or certify the validity of documents (such as a Deed), often by verifying the identification of a person signing a document.

Power of Attorney or P.O.A. A legal document by which you appoint an agent to act for you as Attorney-in-Fact.

Principal. The person who signs a Power of Attorney to appoint an Attorney-in-Fact.

Probate. The court process of validating and administering a Will.

Real Property. Property in the form of land, and buildings or other improvements thereon.

Residue of Your Estate. A term used to describe what property of your Estate is left over and was not specifically given to another person or entity.

Revoke. To destroy the effectiveness of one's Will by executing another or by an act of destruction (as tearing in half).

Self-Proving Affidavit. A form added to a Will, in which the person making the Will and his or her witnesses, swear under oath that they have signed and witnessed the Will; this is overseen by a Notary Public.

Springing Power of Attorney. A Power of Attorney that takes effect upon the occurrence of a specified event, such as the Principal's incapacitation.

Testator. A person who makes a Will.

Testatrix. A woman who makes a Will.

Trustee. The person who manages a Trust; he or she has a legal duty to manage the Trust's assets in the best interest of the Beneficiaries.

Witness. A person who is present, who watches a Principal sign a Will or other document, and signs it as a Witness, to evidence the foregoing.

NOTES

NOTES

NOTES

NOTES

NOTES

NOTES

NOTES

NOTES

NOTES